Next Time You See a
SUNSET

BY EMILY MORGAN

nsta kids
National Science Teaching Association

Arlington, Virginia

National Science Teaching Association

Claire Reinburg, Director
Jennifer Horak, Managing Editor
Andrew Cooke, Senior Editor
Wendy Rubin, Associate Editor
Agnes Bannigan, Associate Editor
Amy America, Book Acquisitions Coordinator

ART AND DESIGN
Will Thomas Jr., Director

PRINTING AND PRODUCTION
Colton Gigot, Senior Production Manager

NATIONAL SCIENCE TEACHERS ASSOCIATION
Gerald F. Wheeler, Executive Director
David Beacom, Publisher

1840 Wilson Blvd., Arlington, VA 22201
www.nsta.org/store
For customer service inquiries, please call 800-277-5300.

Lexile® measure: 630L

Special thanks to Dean Regas, outreach astronomer at the Cincinnati Obervatory Center,
for reviewing this manuscript.

Library of Congress Cataloging-in-Publication Data
Morgan, Emily R. (Emily Rachel), 1973-author.
  Next time you see a sunset / by Emily Morgan.
      p. cm.
Audience: 5-11
  Audience: K to grade 3
  Includes bibliographical references.
  ISBN 978-1-936959-16-7 (print) -- ISBN 978-1-936959-72-3 (e-book) 1. Sun--Rising and setting--Juvenile
literature. 2. Sun--Rotation--Juvenile literature. 3. Atmosphere--Juvenile literature. I. Title.
  QB216.M67 2012
  525'.3--dc23

2012026812

ISBN 978-1-938946-26-4 (library edition)

*For my dad, Jim Stevens,
my very first teacher.*

"Happy is he who gets to know the reasons for things."
—Virgil

A NOTE TO PARENTS AND TEACHERS

The books in this series are intended to be read with a child after she or he has had some experience with the featured objects or phenomena. For example, sit down and watch a sunrise or sunset with your child. (You can find the exact times of sunrise and sunset for any given day in the newspaper or on the internet.) Find a place, without a lot of trees or buildings, where there is a clear view of the western sky. Be sure to bring a flashlight so you can find your way back after the sunset. Watch the colors of the sky change. Discuss what colors you see, how the air temperature feels, and how watching the sunset together makes you feel. Share your ideas and wonderings about what is happening. Why does the sky change color? Why does the Sun look more red or orange than it did earlier that day? Why are your shadows so long?

After you've experienced a sunset or two together, read this book. Take time to pause and share your learnings and wonderings with each other. You will find that new learnings often lead to more questions.

This book does not present facts to be memorized. It was written to inspire a sense of wonder about an ordinary phenomenon and foster a desire to learn more about the natural world. We see sunsets every day and often don't give them a second thought. But when you stop to consider the fact that you are standing on a ball of rock that is turning away from a star into the darkness of space, the experience becomes so much more remarkable. My wish is that after reading this book, you and your child feel a sense of wonder the next time you see a sunset.

—Emily Morgan

*Safety note: Looking directly at the Sun can cause eye damage.

Next time you see a sunset, stop and sit down for a while. Stay very still and watch the sky change.

What colors do you see?

Do the colors change?

Do you feel the air get cooler?

What words would you use to describe the sunset?

How does it make you feel?

Sunsets are some of the most beautiful sights in nature. You might hear people say, "The Sun is 'going down,'" but that's not what is actually happening.

Have you ever wondered what's really going on?

Earth is turning! Earth is rotating, or spinning around, all the time. Earth takes 24 hours to make one complete turn. When you see a sunset, your place on Earth is turning away from our star, the Sun.

As Earth keeps turning, you see less and less of the Sun, until finally you can't see it at all. You see the darkness of space ...

... until the morning, when your place on Earth turns toward our star again. We call this a sunrise, but the Sun is not really rising. It just looks like it is when your place on Earth turns toward it.

The Sun appears in the eastern sky every morning and sets in the western sky each evening because Earth is always turning in the same direction. Most globes have arrows near the equator that point in the direction Earth turns.

If you could look back at Earth from space, you would see that the Sun lights up half of it while the other half is dark. So, while one side of Earth experiences day, the other side experiences night. Along the line between darkness and light are the places on Earth where day changes to night and night changes to day. People in those places are experiencing sunrise or sunset.

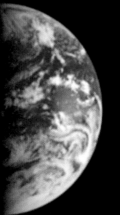

Find your city on a globe. Then find the place directly opposite of your city. Just think, when you see a sunset, the people on the other side of the world see a sunrise. As you are ending your day, they are starting theirs. In fact, the Sun is always "rising" and "setting" somewhere on Earth.

Earth never stops turning. You can sense Earth's spin during the day by watching where the Sun appears in the sky. In the morning, you see the Sun low in the east. As Earth continues to turn, you see the Sun higher in the sky in the middle of the day. In the late afternoon, you see the Sun low in the west.

You can also see evidence
of Earth's spin by watching your
shadow change throughout the day.
Have you ever noticed that your shadow looks
different in the morning and afternoon from
how it looks in the middle of the day? Have you
ever wondered why?

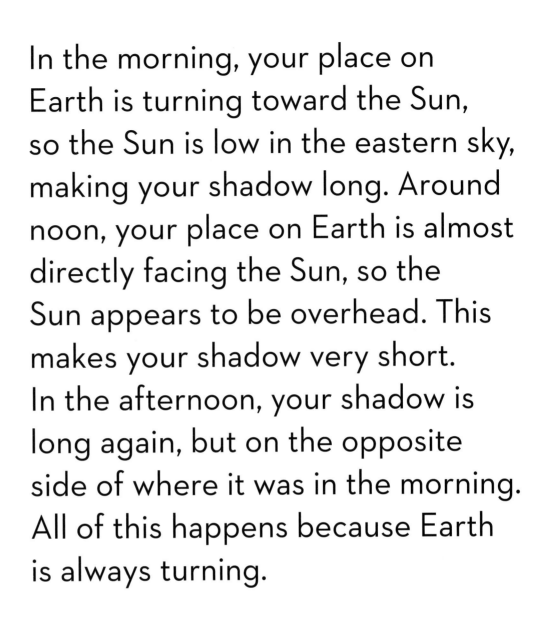

In the morning, your place on
Earth is turning toward the Sun,
so the Sun is low in the eastern sky,
making your shadow long. Around
noon, your place on Earth is almost
directly facing the Sun, so the
Sun appears to be overhead. This
makes your shadow very short.
In the afternoon, your shadow is
long again, but on the opposite
side of where it was in the morning.
All of this happens because Earth
is always turning.

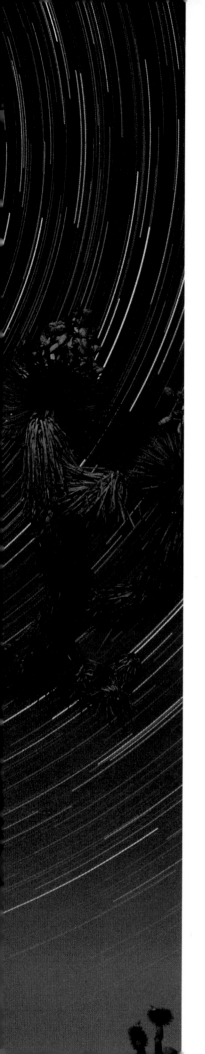

You can even sense Earth's turn at night by watching the stars appear to move across the sky from east to west.

The colors of a sunset can be spectacular. During the day, the sky is blue, but during a sunset, the sky changes to beautiful mixes of orange, pink, red, and yellow. Have you ever wondered why?

As your place on Earth turns away from the Sun, the Sun's light has to travel a longer path through the Earth's atmosphere to get to your eyes. This causes the light to scatter, and only the longer light waves—which are shades of red, orange, and yellow—make it through to your eyes.

So the next time you see a sunset, remember that at that moment, your place on this big ball of rock called Earth is turning away from our beautiful star, the Sun, into the darkness of space. Stay very still as you watch the Sun slowly go out of sight, and know that this is happening because Earth is turning. Isn't that remarkable?

ABOUT THE PHOTOS

Blue Wild Indigo at sunset on the Konza Prairie, Kansas
(Judd Patterson)

Sea stacks and the Pacific Ocean, Oregon
(Judd Patterson)

Summer clouds over the Konza Prairie, Kansas
(Judd Patterson)

A mother and her daughters watch the sunset
on Bethany Beach, Delaware (Katie Hosmer)

Space shuttle *Endeavor*'s view of Earth's horizon
(NASA)

Milky Way over the Flint Hills of Kansas
(Judd Patterson)

Indian grass glowing on the Konza Prairie, Kansas
(Judd Patterson)

Arrow showing the direction Earth turns
(Katie Hosmer)

Earth photographed by *Voyager 1*
(NASA)

Sun shining in New York City
(Katie Hosmer)

30

Sun shining through the trees in Central Park,
New York (Katie Hosmer)

Midday shadows
(Katie Hosmer)

Afternoon shadow
(Katie Hosmer)

The North Star steady above a Joshua tree, California
(Judd Patterson)

Sunset Over Earth, International Space Station
(NASA)

Sundown at Big Cypress National Preserve, Florida
(Judd Patterson)

Spring greenup and sunset on the Konza Prairie,
Kansas (Judd Patterson)

Friends watching the sunset on Bethany Beach,
Delaware (Katie Hosmer)

Activities to Encourage a Sense of Wonder About Sunsets

❖ Observe the sunset several times in the same place. Does it always look the same?

❖ Take a photograph or a video of a sunset.

❖ Bring some art supplies with you to watch the sunset so you can draw or paint it.

❖ Turn the lights out and shine a flashlight on a globe. Be sure to stand back far enough that the flashlight lights half of the globe. Find the arrow on the globe that points in the direction Earth turns, and slowly turn the globe in that direction.

  ❖ Find the places on the globe where there is a line between darkness and light. Those are the places that are experiencing sunrise and sunset when Earth is in that position.

  ❖ Turn the globe and watch the places where sunrise is occurring (the places that are entering the light). Next, find the places on the opposite side of the globe that would be seeing a sunset (the places that are entering darkness as Earth turns).

❖ Go outside in the morning and trace your shadow with chalk. Go out again around noon, stand in the same place, and trace your shadow again. Do this again a third time in the afternoon. How do the outlines of your shadow change throughout the day? When was your shadow the longest? When was it the shortest?

❖ Put a piece of clay on a globe to represent a person. Shine a flashlight on the globe and turn it slowly. Watch the shadow of the clay change throughout the "day." When is the shadow of the clay person the longest? When is it the shortest? Why?

❖ Go to the World Clock website and look at the times in different cities throughout the world. Discuss any patterns you see. Figure out in which cities it is already tomorrow. Find these cities on the globe. Use small sticky notes to label the current time.

Websites

World Clock
www.timeanddate.com/worldclock

Sunrise Sunset: Printable Sunrise/Sunset Calendars
www.sunrisesunset.com

Downloadable classroom activities with student pages can be found at *www.nsta.org/nexttime-sunset*.